U.S. Sites and Symbols

★★★★★★★★★★★★

Historic Buildings

Leia Tait

WEIGL PUBLISHERS INC.

Published by Weigl Publishers Inc.
350 5th Avenue, 59th Floor
New York, NY 10118

Website: www.weigl.com

All of the Internet URLs given in the book were valid at the time of publication. However, due to the dynamic nature of the Internet, some addresses may have changed, or sites may have ceased to exist since publication. While the author and publisher regret any inconvenience this may cause readers, no responsibility for any such changes can be accepted by either the author or the publisher.

Library of Congress Cataloging-in-Publication Data available upon request.
Fax 1-866-44-WEIGL for the attention of the Publishing Records department.

ISBN 978-1-60596-144-6 (hard cover)
ISBN 978-1-60596-145-3 (soft cover)

Printed in the United States of America in North Mankato, Minnesota
2 3 4 5 6 7 8 9 0 14 13 12 11 10

092010
WEP08092010

Editor: Deborah Lambert
Designer: Kathryn Livingstone

Photograph Credits

Every reasonable effort has been made to trace ownership and to obtain permission to reprint copyright material. The publishers would be pleased to have any errors or omissions brought to their attention so that they may be corrected in subsequent printings.

Weigl acknowledges Getty Images as one of its primary image suppliers for this title.

Adams Museum, Deadwood, SD.: page 23 top; Cincinnati Observatory, Chuck Strubbe: page 22 bottom; Daniel Case: page 37 middle; Kenton Rowe/FWP: page 13 top; Library of Congress: pages 10 top, 11 top, 13 bottom, 23 bottom, 28 middle, 28 bottom, 29 bottom, 34 top; Mike Russell: page 20 top; Photo by Alois Mayer: page 37 bottom.

What are Symbols?

A symbol is an item that stands for something else. Objects, artworks, or living things can all be symbols. Every U.S. state has official symbols, or emblems. These items represent the people, history, and culture of the state. State symbols create feelings of pride and citizenship among the people who live there. Each of the 50 U.S. states has official historic buildings. These buildings are a type of official symbol.

National Historic Landmark History

In 1916, the U.S. government created the National Park Service to protect the country's parklands. Nineteen years later, the park service started the National Historic Landmarks Program. This program protects and restores the country's most historic places. Historic buildings represent important people, places, and events in U.S. history. Buildings that are meaningful to all Americans become National Historic Landmarks. Program staff choose the most important sites in the country to become National Historic Landmarks. The first National Historic Landmarks were designated in 1960. Since then, new ones have been added each year. Today, there are more than 2,400 National Historic Landmarks across all 50 states.

The New York Public Library is a National Historic Landmark.

Finding Historic Buildings by Region

Washington

Montana

Oregon

Idaho

Wyoming

The West

Nevada

Utah

Colorado

California

Alaska

Hawai'i

Arizona

New Mexico

Each state has historic buildings. In this book, the states are organized by region. These regions are the West, the Midwest, the South, and the Northeast. Each region is unique because of its land, people, and wildlife. Throughout this book, the regions are color coded. To find a historic building, first find the state using the map on this page. Then, turn to the pages that are the same color as that state.

The Northeast

New Hampshire
Vermont
Maine
Massachusetts
New York
Rhode Island
Connecticut
New Jersey
Delaware
Maryland
Pennsylvania

The Midwest

Minnesota
Wisconsin
Michigan
South Dakota
Iowa
Ohio
Nebraska
Illinois
Indiana
West Virginia
Virginia
Kansas
Missouri
Kentucky

The South

Oklahoma
Arkansas
Tennessee
North Carolina
South Carolina
Georgia
Alabama
Texas
Mississippi
Florida
Louisiana

Web Crawler

Find out facts about each state at **www.americaslibrary.gov**. Click on "Explore the States."

The West

The West is made up of 13 states. They are Alaska, Arizona, California, Colorado, Hawai'i, Idaho, Montana, Nevada, New Mexico, Oregon, Utah, Washington, and Wyoming. Alaska is far to the north. It is separated from the rest of the country by Canada. The Pacific Ocean borders Alaska, Washington, Oregon, and California, and surrounds Hawai'i.

Colorado

Arizona

Hawai'i

The West has many different landforms. There are glaciers in Alaska and volcanoes on Hawai'i. Giant redwood forests grow in Oregon. Deserts cover parts of Arizona, California, Nevada, and Utah. The Rocky Mountains run through Alaska, Washington, Idaho, Montana, Wyoming, Utah, Colorado, and New Mexico.

About 65 million people live in the West. American Indians, Asians, Hispanics, and people of British and German backgrounds make up the largest cultural groups. Nearly four million people live in Los Angeles, California. It is the region's largest city.

Alaska

California

Web Crawler

Discover the Rocky Mountains of the West at **www.blueplanet biomes.org/rocky_mountain.htm**.

Learn more about Hawai'i at www.hawaiikids.net/kids/hawaii_factsnfun.html

Alaska
Alaska Native Brotherhood Hall

The Alaska Native Brotherhood Hall is located in Sitka. Built in 1914, it was the headquarters for the Alaska Native Brotherhood Society. This society was formed to promote equality and legal rights for Alaska's Native Peoples. The group was the first of its kind in Alaska and still exists today. The hall became a National Historic Landmark in 1978.

Arizona
San Xavier del Bac Mission

San Xavier del Bac Mission stands just south of Tucson. Catholic priests built this church in 1797. They came from Spain to teach their religion to the Tohono O'odham people. San Xavier del Bac Mission has many domes, arches, and colorful paintings that blend European and Mexican building styles. The church became a National Historic Landmark in 1960.

California

John Muir House

Martinez, California, is the site of the John Muir House. From 1890 to 1914, this 17-room mansion was the home of John Muir. Muir helped create the Sierra Club, a group that protects nature and wildlife. He was the group's first president. Muir's efforts to protect the environment led to the creation of the National Park Service in 1916. His home became a California Historical Landmark in 1939 and a National Historic Landmark in 1962.

Colorado

United States Air Force Academy, Cadet Area

The United States Air Force Academy, Cadet Area was declared a National Historic Landmark in 2004. One of the most unique buildings at this site is the Cadet Chapel. Built in 1963, the chapel is made of steel, aluminum, and glass. The roof is shaped into 17 spires that have been shaped to look like fighter jets. Inside, there are three chapels, as well as two rooms to serve different religious groups.

Hawai'i
'Iolani Palace

'Iolani Palace was the official home of Hawai'i's last two rulers, King Kalakaua and his sister, Queen Lili'uokalani. Built in 1882, the palace was the center of royal life until the Kingdom of Hawai'i was overthrown in 1893. 'Iolani Palace is the only royal palace ever built in the United States. It became a National Historic Landmark in 1962. Today, it is a museum.

Idaho
Assay Office

The Assay Office is one of the oldest buildings in Boise. It was built in 1871, during the Gold Rush. Miners brought gold, silver, and other metals there to be melted into bars. The bars were returned to the miners or deposited at the office in return for money. Millions of dollars worth of metals passed through the office from 1872 until it closed in 1933. The Assay Office became a National Historic Landmark in 1965. Today, it houses the State Historic Preservation Office and the Archaeological Survey of Idaho.

Montana
Chief Plenty Coups Home

The Chief Plenty Coups Home is in south-central Montana. It was the home of Chief Plenty Coups, the last and best-known chief of the Crow people. Chief Plenty Coups built the home in 1884 and lived there until his death in 1932.

During that time, he was a role model for American Indians living on **reserves**. He showed how they could keep their traditional customs and beliefs even though they settled in one place. Chief Plenty Coups' home became a National Historic Landmark in 1999.

Nevada
Virginia City Historic District

Virginia City was one of the best-known gold-rush towns in the United States.

It looks much the same today as it did in the 1800s. Built in 1877, Storey County Courthouse was the fanciest building of its kind in the state and was very costly to build. It is the oldest courthouse still used in Nevada. The entire city, including the courthouse, was declared a National Historic Landmark in 1961.

New Mexico
Palace of the Governors

Santa Fe is home to the Palace of the Governors. Built in 1610, the palace is the oldest public building in the United States. It became a National Historic Landmark in 1960. Today, the palace houses the state history museum.

Oregon
Pioneer Courthouse

Completed in 1875, the Pioneer Courthouse in Portland was home to the Federal Court and the U.S. Post Office. Since 1973, it has been used by the **U.S. Court of Appeals**. It became a National Historic Landmark in 1977.

Utah
Temple Square

Temple Square is a historic area in Salt Lake City. It became a National Historic Landmark in 1964. The square contains many important buildings of the Mormon Church.

Washington
Pioneer Building, Pergola, and Totem Pole

Henry Yesler was the first millionaire in Seattle, Washington. He built the city's first sawmill, which brought money and jobs to the area. In 1889, a fire destroyed the sawmill and much of the city's downtown. To help rebuild the city, Yesler built an office building where his house had been. It was finished in 1892 and was called the Pioneer Building. Soon, it became an important business location. In 1978, the Pioneer Building was declared a National Historic Landmark.

Wyoming
Old Faithful Inn

The Old Faithful Inn is located in Yellowstone National Park, Wyoming. This inn is the largest log hotel in the world and one of the world's largest log buildings. It is the first National Park building designed to blend in with nature. It became a National Historic Landmark in 1987.

The Midwest

The Midwest is in the center of the United States. It lies between the Rocky Mountains in the west and the Appalachian Mountains in the northeast. The Ohio River separates the Midwest from the South. Canada lies to the north. There are 12 states in the Midwest. They are Illinois, Indiana, Iowa, Kansas, Michigan, Minnesota, Missouri, Nebraska, North Dakota, Ohio, South Dakota, and Wisconsin.

Ohio

South Dakota

The area from North Dakota to Missouri is made up of mostly farming states. They are part of the **Great Plains**. The states from Minnesota to Ohio border the Great Lakes. This chain of freshwater lakes acts as a border between the United States and Canada.

Nearly 65 million people live in the Midwest. There are large groups of African Americans, American Indians, and people of European descent. Many people live in cities. Chicago is the largest city in the Midwest. It is home to three million people. Chicago and other Midwest cities are known for blues, jazz, rap, and rock.

Illinois

Indiana

Web Crawler

Learn everything you need to know about Chicago at **www.explorechicago.org**.

Relive Lewis and Clark's historic trek from the Midwest to the Pacific Ocean at
www.nps.gov/history/nr/travel/lewisandclark

Iowa

Illinois
Abraham Lincoln Home

Abraham Lincoln Home is a historic house in Springfield, Illinois. It is the only house Abraham Lincoln owned. He bought the home in 1841

and lived there with his family until 1861. That year, Lincoln was elected president of the United States and moved to Washington, DC. After his death, the house became a museum. It was named a National Historic Landmark in 1960.

Indiana
Levi Coffin House

The Levi Coffin House is located in Fountain City, Indiana. It was home to Levi and Catharine Coffin, who were part of the

Underground Railroad. They helped slaves escape to Canada and the free states. Hidden rooms in their house gave slaves a safe place to rest. From 1827 to 1847, Levi and Catharine helped more than 2,000 slaves on their journey to freedom. The house became a National Historic Landmark in 1965.

Iowa
Terrace Hill

Des Moines' most important historic building is Terrace Hill. William Boyington designed the home for Benjamin Franklin Allen, Iowa's first millionaire. Terrace Hill was finished in 1869. It measures 18,000 square feet, with three levels and a 90-foot tower. It is well known for its elegant appearance. Since 1977, Terrace Hill has been used as the official home of Iowa's governor. It became a National Historic Landmark in 2003.

Kansas
Sumner Elementary School/ Monroe Elementary School

In 1950, a student named Linda Brown was not allowed to attend a school near her home because she was African

American. She had to go to Monroe Elementary School, 3 miles away. Her father sued the school district, and the court ruled that having separate schools for African Americans was against the U.S. Constitution. Monroe Elementary School and its lands became a National Historic Landmark in 1987.

Michigan
Fisher Building

The Fisher Building is a limestone, granite, and marble skyscraper in Detroit, Michigan. It was designed by Albert Kahn and built in 1928. Many people believe the Fisher Building is one of Kahn's greatest creations. In fact, the building has been called one of the most beautiful skyscrapers ever built in the United States. It became a National Historic Landmark in 1989.

Minnesota
Mayo Clinic Buildings

The Mayo Clinic Buildings are located in Rochester, Minnesota. They were declared a National Historic Landmark in 1969. The Plummer Building was built in 1928, as part of the Mayo Clinic, a not-for-profit medical practice. It soon became a model for hospital buildings across the United States. At 295 feet tall, the Plummer Building was the tallest building in Minnesota until 2001.

Missouri
Mark Twain Boyhood Home

The Mark Twain Boyhood Home is located in Hannibal. It is the childhood home of author

Samuel Clemens, who was better known as Mark Twain. The house and surrounding area inspired many of Twain's novels, including *The Adventures of Tom Sawyer* and *Adventures of Huckleberry Finn*. The house has been a museum since 1912. It became a National Historic Landmark in 1962.

Nebraska
Nebraska State Capitol

The Nebraska State Capitol is in Lincoln. The building was the first to have an office tower. The tower is 400 feet tall, with a domed roof. It is topped with a 19-foot bronze statue. The building at the base of the tower is shaped like a square with a cross inside. It became a National Historic Landmark in 1976.

North Dakota
Fort Union Trading Post

Fort Union Trading Post is on the border between North Dakota and Montana. It was built in 1828 by the American Fur Company. Until 1867, Fort Union was the

most important fur-trading post on the Upper Missouri River. The fort was the longest surviving fur-trading post in the United States. It became a National Historic Landmark in 1961 and a National Historic Site in 1966.

Ohio
Cincinnati Observatory

Opened in 1845, the Cincinnati Observatory is the oldest professional **observatory** in the United States. It soon became

known around the world for the excellent research done by its staff. Their findings helped scientists better understand the Milky Way and develop important theories about space. The observatory became a National Historic Landmark in 1997.

South Dakota
Deadwood Historic District

The Deadwood Historic District became a National Historic Landmark in 1961. After gold was discovered in Deadwood, people flocked to the town. Many buildings were constructed as part of the town's growth, including the W.E. Adams Historic House. Adams became very wealthy selling groceries to people who came to Deadwood during the gold rush. He also served six terms as mayor.

Wisconsin
Pabst Theater

The Pabst Theater in Milwaukee, Wisconsin, is one of the oldest theaters still in use in the United States. It was built in 1895 to house the city's German theater group. Since then, the Pabst has played a major role in the city's theater life. It is also an important symbol of Milwaukee's German-American heritage. The Pabst Theater is an official City of Milwaukee Landmark and a State of Wisconsin Historical Site. It became a National Historic Landmark in 1991.

The South

The South is made up of 16 states. They are Alabama, Arkansas, Delaware, Florida, Georgia, Kentucky, Louisiana, Maryland, Mississippi, North Carolina, Oklahoma, South Carolina, Tennessee, Texas, Virginia, and West Virginia. The Atlantic Ocean borders the South from Delaware to the tip of Florida. A part of the Atlantic Ocean called the Gulf of Mexico stretches from Florida's west coast to Texas. Mexico lies to the south.

Florida

Alabama

The South is known for its warm weather. It also has plenty of rain. This makes it easy for plants to grow. In the past, cotton, tobacco, rice, and sugarcane were important crops in the South. They shaped southern history.

More than 100 million people live in the South. About 20 million are African American. Many people of Hispanic and European backgrounds also live there. Together, southerners share a special history and culture. Blues, gospel, rock, and country music all began in the South. Many well-known writers, such as Tennessee Williams, have lived there. The South is also known for its barbeque, Tex-Mex, and Cajun cooking.

Texas

West Virginia

Web Crawler

Learn the best places to
see Southern wildlife at
www.iexplore.com/usmap/South/s_bird/Safari.

Explore **civil rights** landmarks in the South at
www.nps.gov/history/nr/travel/civilrights/mainmap.htm

Mississippi

Alabama
Brown Chapel A.M.E. Church

In 1965, African Americans taking part in a march from Brown Chapel in Selma to Montgomery were attacked by state troops. The day, known as "Bloody Sunday," led to the passing of the **Voting Rights Act**. The church became a National Historic Landmark in 1997.

Arkansas
Little Rock Central High School

In 1957, African Americans were allowed to attend

this school for the first time. The governor sent troops to stop them, but President Eisenhower sent other troops to escort the students inside. The school became a National Historic Landmark in 1982.

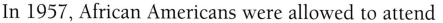

Delaware
Holy Trinity (Old Swedes) Church

Holy Trinity (Old Swedes) Church was built in 1698 over part of the first Swedish

settlement in North America. It became a National Historic Landmark in 1961. It is one of the oldest churches in the country.

Florida
Freedom Tower

Freedom Tower in Miami was built in 1925 to house the city's newspaper, *Miami News*. In 1962, the U.S. government made the tower a welcome center for Cuban immigrants. It became a National Historic Landmark in 2008.

Georgia
Martin Luther King, Jr. Historic District

The Martin Luther King, Jr. Historic District in Atlanta became a National Historic Landmark in 1977. Civil rights leader Martin Luther King, Jr. was born here on January 15, 1929.

Kentucky
United States Marine Hospital

The United States Marine Hospital opened in Louisville in 1852 and is the best surviving example of a hospital built before the **Civil War**. It became a National Historic Landmark in 1997.

Louisiana
The Cabildo

Located in New Orleans, the Cabildo originally housed the Spanish government that ruled Louisiana. In 1803, the Cabildo was the official site of the **Louisiana Purchase**. The Cabildo became a National Historic Landmark in 1960.

Maryland
Clara Barton House

Clara Barton founded the American Red Cross in 1881. In 1897, a Red Cross warehouse in Glen Echo became her home and the American Red Cross headquarters. The house became a National Historic Landmark in 1965.

Mississippi
Mississippi Governor's Mansion

The Mississippi Governor's Mansion is a historic building in Jackson. Completed in 1841, it is the second-oldest governor's mansion in use today. The mansion became a National Historic Landmark in 1975.

North Carolina
Cape Hatteras Light Station

The Cape Hatteras Light Station is the tallest lighthouse in the United States. It was built in 1870 to protect sailors in the dangerous waters of Cape Hatteras, known as the "Graveyard of the Atlantic." The 208-foot-tall lighthouse is painted with black and white spiral bands. Many people visit the lighthouse each year. It became a National Historic Landmark in 1998.

Oklahoma
Cherokee National Capitol

Tahlequah, Oklahoma, is the site of the Cherokee National Capitol. This brick building was the council house of the Cherokee Nation from 1869 to 1907. Later, it became the Cherokee County Courthouse. The building was declared a National Historic Landmark in 1961.

South Carolina
Exchange and Provost

The Exchange and Provost building in Charleston was built in 1771. It began as a public meeting place, as well as a custom house, where taxes on imported items were collected. During the **American Revolution**, the building was

used as a British military prison. In 1791, the state's new constitution was signed here. The following year, President George Washington visited the building. It became a National Historic Landmark in 1973.

Tennessee
Graceland

One of best-known historic buildings in the United States is Graceland in Memphis, Tennessee. Graceland was the home of music legend Elvis Presley from 1957 to 1977. After his death, the mansion became a museum. It contains many of Elvis' belongings and awards. Graceland became a National Historic Landmark in 2006. It is the second most-visited house museum in the United States, after the White House.

Texas
Alamo

Built in 1724, the Alamo is a mission and fortress in San Antonio. Many battles took place here between the Mexican and Texan armies in the early 1800s. More than four million people visit the Alamo every year. It became a National Historic Landmark in 1960.

Virginia
Pentagon

Located in Arlington, the Pentagon was completed in 1943 and was used as the U.S. War Office. At the time, it was the largest office building in the country. Today, the Pentagon is home to the U.S. Department of Defense. It became a National Historic Landmark in 1992.

West Virginia
The Greenbrier

People began visiting the natural hot spring in White Sulphur Springs in 1778. The Greenbrier, a hotel, was built there in 1913. Many U.S. presidents have stayed there. The Greenbrier became a National Historic Landmark in 1990.

The Northeast

The Northeast is the smallest region in the United States. It is east of the Great Lakes and south of Canada. The Atlantic Ocean borders the Northeast coast. There are nine states in the Northeast. They are Connecticut, Maine, Massachusetts, New Hampshire, New Jersey, New York, Pennsylvania, Rhode Island, and Vermont.

Connecticut

Vermont

Many natural wonders are found in the Northeast. The Appalachian Mountains stretch through Maine, New Hampshire, Vermont, New York, and Pennsylvania. Lake Erie and Lake Ontario border New York. Niagara Falls flows between them. Half of Niagara Falls is located in the United States. The other half is located in Canada. On the U.S. side, the falls are 1,000 feet wide and 167 feet tall.

In the 1600s, the first settlers from Europe came to the area known as **New England**. Today, 55 million people live in the Northeast. More Irish Americans and Italian Americans live here than in any other part of the country. More than eight million people live in New York City, the largest city in the country.

Maine

New York

Web Crawler

Visit important presidential sites in the Northeast at **www.nps.gov/ history/nr/travel/presidents/map_northeast.html**.

Discover the Northeast's natural wonders by clicking on the states at **www.nps.gov**

Pennsylvania

Connecticut

Connecticut Hall

Connecticut Hall is the oldest building in New Haven, Connecticut, and on the campus of Yale University. Yale is the third-oldest U.S. university. It was founded in 1701. Connecticut Hall was completed in 1753. It was the school's first brick building. Today, it is the only building remaining from Yale's early period. It became a National Historic Landmark in 1965.

Maine

Wadsworth-Longfellow House

The first brick house in Portland, Maine, was the Wadsworth-Longfellow House. Built in 1786, it was the birthplace and childhood home of Henry Wadsworth-Longfellow. Wadsworth-Longfellow became the best-known U.S. poet of the 19th century. The house became National Historic Landmark in 1962.

Massachusetts
Faneuil Hall

Faneuil Hall is a marketplace and meeting hall in Boston. Built in 1742, the hall was an important place in the days leading up to the American Revolution. It is often called "the home of free speech" and "the cradle of liberty." The first town meeting was held here. Patriots, such as Samuel Adams and John Otis, made important speeches at the hall. It became a National Historic Landmark in 1960.

New Hampshire
Augustus Saint-Gaudens Memorial

Augustus Saint-Gaudens was one of the best-known sculptors in the United States. Saint-Gaudens lived in this house in Cornish from 1885 to 1907. Many of his belongings are still found at the house. His sculptures are displayed in the home's gardens and an on-site gallery. The house became a National Historic Landmark in 1962.

New Jersey
Albert Einstein House

Alberta Einstein House is located in Princeton, New Jersey. It is the historic home of physicist Albert Einstein. Einstein lived in the house from 1936 until his death in 1955. It was named a National Historic Landmark in 1976.

New York
Empire State Building

Built in 1931, the Empire State Building is one of the world's best-known buildings. Construction began on the structure in January 1930, and it took 7,000,000 hours of human labor to build. At 1,454 feet, it was the world's tallest building for 41 years. The Empire State Building has been called one of the seven wonders of the modern world. It became a National Historic Landmark in 1986.

Pennsylvania
First Bank of the United States

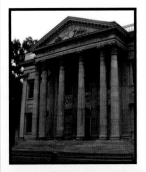

The First Bank of the United States was chartered in 1791 for 20 years. It was built to handle the central government's banking needs after the American Revolution. The bank was built in Philadelphia, the U.S. capital at that time. It became a National Historic Landmark in 1987.

Rhode Island
Crescent Park Looff Carousel

Built in 1895, the Crescent Park Looff Carousel is found in East Providence. The carousel has 62 hand-carved figures and four chariots. It became a National Historic Landmark in 1987.

Vermont
Calvin Coolidge Homestead District

Plymouth Notch is the childhood home of Calvin Coolidge. When President Harding died in 1923, Coolidge's father swore his son in as president in the home's sitting room. The house and its surroundings became a National Historic Landmark in 1965.

A National Historic Building

National emblems are symbols that are used for the entire country. The American flag, known as the star-spangled banner, is one such symbol. Another is the bald eagle, which is the national bird. The oak tree is the national tree. One of the best-known national historic buildings in the United States is the White House.

The White House has six floors. The First Family lives on the top two floors.

The president works in the Oval Office in the West Wing.

The two middle floors are open to the public. Visitors can tour historic rooms, such as the Blue Room and the State Dining Room.

History of the White House

The White House was built from 1792 to 1800. Building began when George Washington was president, but John Adams was the first president to live there. Every president, since Adams, has lived in the White House.

Guide to Historic Buildings

A NATIONAL HISTORIC BUILDING
The White House

ALABAMA
Brown Chapel A.M.E. Church

ALASKA
Alaska Native Brotherhood Hall

ARIZONA
San Xavier del Bac Mission

ARKANSAS
Little Rock Central High School

CALIFORNIA
John Muir House

COLORADO
United States Air Force Academy, Cadet Area

CONNECTICUT
Hall

DELAWARE
Holy Trinity (Old Swedes) Church

FLORIDA
Freedom Tower

GEORGIA
Martin Luther King, Jr. Historic District

HAWAI'I
'Iolani Palace

IDAHO
Assay Office

ILLINOIS
Abraham Lincoln Home

INDIANA
Levi Coffin House

IOWA
Terrace Hill

KANSAS
Sumner/Monroe Elementary School

KENTUCKY
United States Marine Hospital

LOUISIANA
The Cabildo

MAINE
Wadsworth-Longfellow House

MARYLAND
Clara Barton House

MASSACHUSETTS
Faneuil Hall

MICHIGAN
Fisher Building

MINNESOTA
Mayo Clinic
Buildings

MISSISSIPPI
Mississippi
Governor's
Mansion

MISSOURI
Mark Twain
Boyhood Home

MONTANA
Chief Plenty
Coups Home

NEBRASKA
Nebraska State
Capitol

NEVADA
Virginia City
Historic District

NEW HAMPSHIRE
Augustus
Saint-Gaudens
Memorial

NEW JERSEY
Albert Einstein
House

NEW MEXICO
Palace of the
Governors

NEW YORK
The Empire
State Building

**NORTH
CAROLINA**
Cape Hatteras
Light Station

**NORTH
DAKOTA**
Fort Union
Trading Post

OHIO
Cincinnati
Observatory

OKLAHOMA
Cherokee
National
Capitol

OREGON
Pioneer
Courthouse

PENNSYLVANIA
First Bank of the
United States

RHODE ISLAND
Crescent Park
Looff Carousel

**SOUTH
CAROLINA**
Exchange and
Provost

**SOUTH
DAKOTA**
Deadwood
Historic District

TENNESSEE
Graceland

TEXAS
Alamo

UTAH
Temple Square

VERMONT
Calvin Coolidge
Homestead
District

VIRGINIA
The Pentagon

WASHINGTON
Pioneer Building,
Pergola, and
Totem Pole

**WEST
VIRGINIA**
The Greenbrier

WISCONSIN
Pabst Theater

WYOMING
Old Faithful
Inn

Parts of Historic Buildings

O nly the most important historic buildings, such as the Library of Congress in Washington, DC, become National Historic Landmarks. Those that are chosen usually fall into one of the five categories on this page.

PEOPLE Some National Historic Landmarks are linked to important people. These people are remembered in the buildings where they lived or worked.

EVENTS Many buildings that become National Historic Landmarks were once the scene of important events. Visiting these buildings helps people understand how certain events shaped the country's history.

WAY OF LIFE Some buildings that become National Historic Landmarks show how certain people or groups lived in the past. These buildings are usually connected to cultural groups.

IDEALS Some National Historic buildings represent American ideals, such as freedom and equality. These ideals may be symbolized in the events that occurred in these buildings, their design features, or other aspects.

DESIGN Many buildings become National Historic Landmarks because of their special design or construction. These buildings are often outstanding examples of craftsmanship. They also show how people lived and worked in the past.

Test Your Knowledge

1 Which president was sworn into office at his childhood home?

2 What region is home to the historic Connecticut Hall (Connecticut) and Faneuil Hall (Massachusetts)?

3 What two historic schools were important to the U.S. civil rights movement?

4 How many historic buildings in this book are churches or religious buildings?

5 What type of historic building is found in Rhode Island?

6 What is similar about the Freedom Tower in Florida and the State Capitol in Nebraska?

7 What region is home to the U.S. Marine Hospital of Louisville, the Cape Hatteras Light Station, the Exchange and Provost, the Pentagon, and the Greenbrier?

8 What type of historic building is shown for both Oregon and Nevada?

9 Which state has a trading post as a historic building?

13 Where is the oldest professional observatory in the United States?

10 The Assay Office, the Pioneer Building, and the Old Faithful Inn can all be found in what region?

14 What Milwaukee building is an important German-American landmark?

11 Where was the First Bank of the United States built?

15 Which state is home to the second-oldest governor's mansion still in use today?

12 What state is home to the only royal palace in the United States?

Designate a Historic Building

Designate a building to represent you and your achievements. Begin by thinking about the buildings that are important in your life. Use the examples in this book to help you. Were you born in a special building? What places do you visit every day? Think about the major events in your life. Where did they take place?

Write a description of your building. What kind of building is it? What does it look like? When was it built? Where is it located? Why is it important to you? What will others learn about you by visiting this building?

Take a photo or draw a picture of your building. Attach the picture to your description. Then, share it with your friends. What kinds of buildings did they choose? What do their choices tell you about them?

Further Research

Many books and websites provide information on historic buildings. To learn more about historic buildings, borrow books from the library, or surf the Internet.

Books

Most libraries have computers that connect to a database for researching information. If you input a key word, you will be provided with a list of books in the library that contain information on that topic. Non-fiction books are arranged numerically, using their call number. Fiction books are organized alphabetically by the author's last name.

Websites

Find fun facts about each of the 50 U.S. states by clicking on the map from the U.S. Census Bureau found at **www.census.gov/schools/facts**.

Take the Great American Landmarks Adventure at **www.nps.gov/history/hps/pad/adventure/tripintro.htm**.

Read more about the regions of the United States at **www.factmonster.com/ipka/A0770177.html**.

See photos and drawings of historic U.S. buildings at **http://lcweb2.loc.gov/ammem/collections/habs_haer/hhmap01.html#als**.

Glossary

American Revolution: a war that took place from 1775 to 1783, in which the American colonies won their independence from Great Britain

civil rights: basic freedoms and privileges guaranteed to all citizens

Civil War: a war between the northern and southern states, from 1861 to 1865

Great Plains: a vast grassland region covering 10 U.S. states and 4 Canadian provinces. Used for farming and raising cattle

Louisiana Purchase: 828,000 square miles of land bought by the United States from France in 1803

New England: the most northeastern U.S. states—Connecticut, Rhode Island, Vermont, Massachusetts, New Hampshire, and Maine

observatory: a building that has a telescope and other scientific equipment

reserves: areas of land set aside for use by American Indians

Underground Railroad: a secret network of people who helped slaves from the southern United States make their way north to freedom

U.S. Court of Appeals: a special court that reviews decisions made in district courts and special court cases

Voting Rights Act: a law making it illegal for states to use literacy tests, taxes, or other obstacles to keep African Americans from voting

Index